Every

contents

Quick Chicken Parmesan

Makes 4 servings

PREP TIME
5 minutes

BAKE TIME
25 minutes

4 skinless, boneless chicken breast halves (about
    1 pound)

2 cups Prego® Traditional Italian Sauce *or* Fresh
    Mushroom Italian Sauce

2 ounces shredded mozzarella cheese (about ½ cup)

2 tablespoons grated Parmesan cheese

½ of a 16-ounce package spaghetti, cooked and
    drained (about 4 cups)

1. Place the chicken in a 2-quart shallow baking dish. Top the chicken with the Italian sauce. Sprinkle with the mozzarella cheese and Parmesan cheese.

2. Bake at 400°F. for 25 minutes or until cooked through. Serve with the spaghetti.

Turkey & Broccoli Alfredo

Makes 4 servings

PREP TIME
10 minutes

COOK TIME
20 minutes

½ package (8 ounces) linguine

1 cup fresh *or* frozen broccoli flowerets

1 can (10¾ ounces) Campbell's® Condensed Cream of Mushroom Soup (Regular *or* 98% Fat Free)

½ cup milk

½ cup grated Parmesan cheese

¼ teaspoon ground black pepper

2 cups cubed cooked turkey

Kitchen Tip

Substitute spaghetti for the linguine.

1. Prepare the linguine according to the package directions in a 3-quart saucepan. Add the broccoli during the last 4 minutes of the cooking time. Drain the linguine mixture well in a colander. Return the linguine mixture to the saucepan.

2. Stir the soup, milk, cheese, black pepper and turkey in the saucepan and cook over medium heat until the mixture is hot and bubbling, stirring occasionally. Serve with additional Parmesan cheese.

Crunchy Chicken and Gravy

Makes 4 servings

PREP TIME
10 minutes

BAKE TIME
20 minutes

COOK TIME
5 minutes

1 cup Pepperidge Farm® Herb Seasoned Stuffing, crushed

2 tablespoons grated Parmesan cheese

1 egg

4 skinless, boneless chicken breast halves (about 1 pound)

2 tablespoons butter, melted

1 jar (12 ounces) Campbell's® Slow Roast Chicken Gravy

1. Stir the stuffing and cheese on a plate. Beat the egg in a shallow dish with a fork or whisk. Dip the chicken into the egg. Coat the chicken with the stuffing mixture. Place the chicken onto a baking sheet. Drizzle with the butter.

2. Bake at 400°F. for 20 minutes or until the chicken is cooked through.

3. Heat the gravy in a 1-quart saucepan over medium heat until hot and bubbling. Serve the gravy with the chicken.

Quick & Easy Chicken Quesadillas

Makes 8 servings

PREP TIME
15 minutes

COOK TIME
15 minutes

BAKE TIME
5 minutes

4 skinless, boneless chicken breast halves
    (about 1 pound), cut into cubes

1 can (10¾ ounces) Campbell's® Condensed Cream
    of Chicken Soup (Regular *or* 98% Fat Free)

½ cup Pace® Picante Sauce

½ cup shredded Monterey Jack cheese

1 teaspoon chili powder

8 flour tortillas (8-inch), warmed

1. Heat the oven to 425°F.

2. Cook the chicken in a 10-inch nonstick skillet over medium-high heat until well browned and cooked through, stirring often. Stir in the soup, picante sauce, cheese and chili powder and cook until the mixture is hot and bubbling.

3. Place the tortillas onto **2** baking sheets. Spread **about ⅓ cup** chicken mixture on **half** of **each** tortilla to within ½ inch of the edge. Brush the edges of the tortillas with water. Fold the tortillas over the filling and press the edges to seal.

4. Bake for 5 minutes or until the filling is hot. Cut the quesadillas into wedges.

Barbecued Chicken Sandwiches

Makes 4 servings

PREP TIME
10 minutes

COOK TIME
15 minutes

1 tablespoon butter

1 small green pepper, chopped (about ½ cup) (optional)

1 small onion, chopped (about ¼ cup)

¼ cup chopped celery

½ cup barbecue sauce

2 cans (4.5 ounces *each*) Swanson® Premium White Chunk Chicken Breast in Water, drained

4 Pepperidge Farm® Farmhouse Premium White Rolls with Sesame Seeds, split and toasted

1. Heat the butter in a 2-quart saucepan over medium heat. Stir the pepper, onion and celery in the saucepan and cook until they're tender.

2. Stir the barbecue sauce and chicken in the saucepan. Heat until the mixture is hot and bubbling. Divide the chicken mixture among the rolls.

Cheesy Chicken Pizza

Makes 4 servings

PREP TIME
15 minutes

BAKE TIME
15 minutes

1 package (about 13 ounces) refrigerated pizza dough

½ cup Pace® Picante Sauce

½ cup Prego® Traditional Italian Sauce *or* Roasted Garlic & Herb Italian Sauce

1 cup chopped cooked chicken *or* turkey

½ cup sliced pitted ripe olives

2 green onions, sliced (about ¼ cup)

4 ounces shredded mozzarella cheese (about 1 cup)

Kitchen Tip

For a crispier crust, prepare the dough as directed in step 2. Bake the dough for 5 minutes. Remove the dough from the oven and proceed as directed in steps 3 and 4.

1. Heat the oven to 425°F.

2. Unroll the dough onto a greased 12-inch pizza pan. Press the dough into a 12-inch circle. Pinch up the edge to form a rim.

3. Stir the picante sauce and Italian sauce in a small bowl. Spread the picante sauce mixture over the crust to the rim. Top with the chicken, olives, onions and cheese.

4. Bake for 15 minutes or until the cheese is melted and the crust is golden brown.

Creamy Pork Marsala with Fettuccine

Makes 4 servings

PREP TIME
5 minutes

COOK TIME
25 minutes

1 tablespoon olive oil

4 boneless pork chops, ¾-inch thick (about 1 pound)

1 cup sliced mushrooms (about 3 ounces)

1 clove garlic, minced

1 can (10¾ ounces) Campbell's® Condensed Cream of Mushroom Soup (Regular *or* 98% Fat Free)

½ cup milk

2 tablespoons dry Marsala wine

8 ounces spinach fettuccine, cooked and drained

Kitchen **Tip**

Marsalas can range from dry to sweet, so be sure to use a dry one for this recipe.

1. Heat the oil in a 10-inch skillet over medium-high heat. Add the pork and cook until it's well browned on both sides.

2. Reduce the heat to medium. Add the mushrooms and garlic to the skillet and cook until the mushrooms are tender.

3. Stir the soup, milk and wine in the skillet and heat to a boil. Reduce the heat to low. Cover and cook for 5 minutes or until the pork is cooked through. Serve the pork and sauce with the pasta.

Bistro Onion Burgers

Makes 6 servings

PREP TIME
5 minutes

COOK TIME
10 minutes

1½ pounds ground beef

1 envelope (about 1 ounce) dry onion soup and
   recipe mix

3 tablespoons water

6 Pepperidge Farm® Farmhouse Premium White
   Rolls with Sesame Seeds, split and toasted

   Lettuce leaves
   Tomato slices

1. Thoroughly mix the beef, soup mix and water. Shape the beef mixture into **6** (½-inch-thick) burgers.

2. Cook the burgers in batches in a 10-inch skillet over medium-high heat until well browned on both sides, 10 minutes for medium or to desired doneness.

3. Serve the burgers on the rolls. Top with the lettuce and tomato.

Pork Tenderloin with Peach & Pecan Sauce

Makes 4 servings

PREP TIME
20 minutes

COOK TIME
20 minutes

1 tablespoon olive oil

1 pork tenderloin (about 1 pound), cut into ¾-inch-thick slices

2 cloves garlic, minced

2 green onions, sliced (about ¼ cup)

1 can (10¾ ounces) Campbell's® Condensed Golden Mushroom Soup

1 can (about 15 ounces) sliced peaches in juice, drained, reserving juice

3 tablespoons low-sodium soy sauce

2 tablespoons honey

¼ cup pecan halves, toasted and broken into large pieces

Hot cooked rice

1. Heat the oil in a 10-inch skillet over medium-high heat. Add the pork and cook until well browned on both sides. Remove the pork from the skillet.

2. Add the garlic and onions to the skillet and cook and stir for 1 minute. Stir the soup, peach juice, soy sauce and honey in the skillet and heat to a boil. Cook for 5 minutes or until the soup mixture is slightly reduced.

3. Return the pork to the skillet. Stir in the peaches. Reduce the heat to low. Cook until the pork is cooked through. Stir in the pecans. Serve the pork and sauce with the rice. Sprinkle with additional sliced green onion, if desired.

Soft Tacos

Makes 8 servings

PREP TIME
10 minutes

COOK TIME
15 minutes

1 **pound ground beef**

1 **tablespoon chili powder**

1 **cup Pace® Picante Sauce**

8 **flour tortillas (8-inch), warmed**

1 **cup shredded lettuce**

1 **cup shredded Cheddar cheese**

1. Cook beef and chili powder in a 10-inch skillet over medium-high heat until the beef is well browned, stirring often to separate the meat. Pour off any fat.

2. Stir the picante sauce in the skillet and cook until the mixture is hot and bubbling.

3. Spoon **about ¼ cup** beef mixture down the center of **each** tortilla. Top with the lettuce and cheese. Fold the tortillas around the filling. Serve with additional picante sauce.

Mushroom-Smothered Beef Burgers

Makes 4 servings

PREP TIME
15 minutes

COOK TIME
25 minutes

1 can (10¾ ounces) Campbell's® Condensed Cream of Mushroom Soup (Regular *or* 98% Fat Free)
1 pound ground beef
⅓ cup Italian-seasoned dry bread crumbs
1 small onion, finely chopped (about ¼ cup)
1 egg, beaten
1 tablespoon vegetable oil
1 tablespoon Worcestershire sauce
2 tablespoons water
1½ cups sliced mushrooms (about 4 ounces)

Kitchen Tip

You can substitute ground turkey for the ground beef in this recipe.

1. Thoroughly mix ¼ **cup** soup, beef, bread crumbs, onion and egg in a large bowl. Shape the beef mixture firmly into **4** (½-inch-thick) burgers.

2. Heat the oil in a 10-inch skillet over medium-high heat. Add the burgers and cook until they're well browned on both sides. Pour off any fat.

3. Add the remaining soup, Worcestershire, water and mushrooms to the skillet and heat to a boil. Reduce the heat to low. Cover and cook for 10 minutes or until the burgers are cooked through.

Quick Spaghetti & Meatballs

Makes 6 servings

PREP TIME
5 minutes

COOK TIME
25 minutes

1 jar (45 ounces) Prego® Flavored with Meat
   Italian Sauce

16 frozen meatballs (1 ounce *each*)

1 package (16-ounce) spaghetti, cooked and
   drained (about 8 cups)
   Grated Parmesan cheese

1. Stir the Italian sauce and meatballs in 3-quart saucepan and heat to a boil over medium heat. Reduce the heat to low. Cover and cook for 20 minutes or until the meatballs are heated through, stirring occasionally.

2. Serve the sauce and meatballs over the spaghetti. Sprinkle with the cheese.

Polynesian Burgers

Makes 6 servings

PREP TIME
10 minutes

COOK TIME
20 minutes

1½ pounds ground beef

1 can (8 ounces) pineapple slices in juice, undrained

1 can (10½ ounces) Campbell's® Condensed French Onion Soup

2 teaspoons packed brown sugar

1 tablespoon cider vinegar

1 loaf French bread, cut crosswise into 6 pieces

1. Shape the beef into **6** (½-inch-thick) burgers.

2. Cook the burgers in a 12-inch skillet over medium-high heat until well browned on both sides. Pour off any fat. Top **each** burger with **1** slice pineapple. Reserve the pineapple juice.

3. Stir the soup, reserved pineapple juice, brown sugar and vinegar in a small bowl. Add the soup mixture to the skillet and heat to a boil. Reduce the heat to low. Cover and cook for 5 minutes or until the burgers are cooked through.

4. Split the bread pieces. Serve the burgers and sauce on the bread.

Baked Potatoes Olé

Makes 4 servings

PREP TIME
5 minutes

COOK TIME
15 minutes

1 **pound ground beef**
1 **tablespoon chili powder**
1 **cup Pace® Picante Sauce**
4 **hot baked potatoes, split**
   Shredded Cheddar cheese

Kitchen **Tip**

To bake the potatoes, pierce the potatoes with a fork. Bake at 400°F. for 1 hour or microwave on HIGH for 12 minutes or until fork-tender.

1. Cook the beef and chili powder in a 10-inch skillet over medium-high heat until the beef is well browned, stirring often to separate the meat. Pour off any fat.

2. Stir the picante sauce in the skillet. Reduce the heat to low. Cook until the mixture is hot and bubbling. Serve the beef mixture over the potatoes. Top with the cheese.